Contents

Life in the desert

A dry desert landscape in the south-western USA.

Deserts are extreme places. They can be very hot during the day and very cold at night. They can also be very dry. In South America's Atacama Desert, for example, it only rained four times in one hundred years.

Extreme landscapes

The landscape of the desert is affected by the great range of temperatures. Very few plants can survive in such a wide range of hot, dry and cold conditions. Some landscapes are simply made up of endless sand dunes or large rocks. Only a few types of grass, trees or bushes can be found growing there.

Yummy!

The camel spider lives in deserts around the world and can grow up to 15 cm long. It likes to catch and eat lizards and small birds.

Survival

Because deserts are such extreme places, the plants, animals and people that live there have to depend on each other in order to survive.

In the Sahara Desert in Africa – the largest desert on Earth – goats survive by eating such grasses as are available. In turn, people living there, known as Bedouins, drink goats' milk.

Who eats who in the Desert?

Andrew Campbell

FRANKLIN WATTS
LONDON•SYDNEY

This edition 2009

Copyright © 2005 Franklin Watts

Franklin Watts
338 Euston Road
London NW1 3BH

Franklin Watts Australia
Level 17/207 Kent Street
Sydney, NSW 2000

All rights reserved.

A CIP catalogue record for this book is
available from the British Library.

Dewey number: 577.54

ISBN 978 0 7496 8907 0

Printed in Malaysia

Franklin Watts is a division of
Hachette Children's books, an Hachette
Livre UK company.
www.hachettelivre.co.uk

Designer: Cali Roberts
Editor: Constance Novis
Art Director: Peter Scoulding
Editor-in-Chief: John C. Miles
Picture Research: Diana Morris
Artwork: Ian Thompson

Note to parents and teachers
Every effort has been made by the Publishers to ensure that the
websites in this book are suitable for children, that they are of
the highest educational value, and that they contain no
inappropriate or offensive material. However, because of the
nature of the Internet, it is impossible to guarantee that the
contents of these sites will not be altered. We strongly advise
that Internet access is supervised by a responsible adult.

PICTURE CREDITS

John Calcalosi/Still Pictures: 9, 16bl, 21, 24
Brian Cushing/Ecoscene: 14
Michele Depraz/Still Pictures: 12
Nigel J Dennis/Still Pictures: 27
Xavier Eichaker/Still Pictures: 6, 15, 17
M & P Fogden/FLPA: 7
Klein/Hubert/Still Pictures: 4b
Wayne Lawler/Ecoscene: 18, 19
Wyman Meinzer/Still Pictures: front cover, 1, 22
C. Allan Morgan/Still Pictures: 25
Michael Rauch/Still Pictures: 13
Ed Reschke/Still Pictures: 11
Francois Sauveny/Still Pictures: 26
Roland Seitre/Still Pictures: 8
Raoul Slater/WWI/Still Pictures: 10
Tom Vezo/Still Pictures: 20
Gordon Wiltsie/Still Pictures: 5t, 16tr
Gunter Ziesler/Still Pictures: 23

*Every attempt has been made to clear copyright. Should
there be any inadvertent omission please apply to the
publisher for rectification.*

We're in the chain!

Nomads are people who have survived in deserts for thousands of years. In Africa, nomads such as the Bedouin people keep herds of goats and camels, which they rely on for milk and meat.

Habitats and food chains

All organisms (living things) require a place to live where they can find everything necessary for survival. This place is known as a habitat. Within every habitat exist food chains. These are simple lists showing the links between who eats what, or whom. By looking at a food chain you can see how each part of the chain helps to keep the next part alive.

Who Eats Who?

grass

The moloch lizard, or thorny devil, of Australia has adapted to survive in one of the world's most extreme environments.

goat

Bedouin drinks goat's milk

From chains to webs

A food chain shows how one animal eats one type of plant, or one other animal. But in the desert, where there might be little food, most animals have to eat whatever they can find. This means they depend on lots of different plants and animals – a relationship called a food web.

Yummy!

The Australian skink, a type of lizard that lives in the desert, has a very mixed diet. It eats spiders, cockroaches, centipedes, beetles, termites, ants, grasshoppers, crickets and silverfish.

Houbara bustard

A food web in action

A food web shows how different food chains are connected. For example, the houbara bustard, which lives in the deserts of Central Asia, is part of many different food chains. This is because it eats plant seeds and shoots as well as locusts, beetles and lizards.

All these animals can be linked together in a food web. If the bustard could not find seeds, it might eat more beetles. This would leave fewer beetles for animals in other food chains to eat.

A desert yucca moth perches on a yucca flower.

We're in the chain!

Aborigines in Australia have traditionally eaten the witchetty grub, a type of caterpillar that lives in the roots of the acacia bush. Aborigines eat the grub raw or cook it in ashes.

Wet and dry webs

Weather has a great effect on food chains and food webs in the desert. In very dry weather, a lizard might eat seeds or small insects. When rain does finally arrive, plants burst into life and grow. Animals breed or travel into the desert to look for food, which gives the lizard more choice in what it eats.

Fussy eaters

Most desert animals eat whatever they can. However, some creatures are fussy. In the deserts of the USA, for example, the yucca moth only eats the yucca plant; the female moth lays its eggs on the plant. But the yucca plant depends on the yucca moth, too. Every time the female visits a yucca plant it spreads pollen from one yucca to another. This allows the yucca plant to reproduce.

Desert plants

Plants are the first link in any food chain, since they make their energy directly from sunlight through photosynthesis. This energy is available to other living things higher up the food chain.

Strong sunlight

Unlike plants elsewhere, desert plants face a unique problem – too much sunlight! In strong sunlight people often wear light-coloured clothes that reflect the sun and keep them cool. Many desert plants use the same idea. They have pale green or grey stems and branches to reflect the sunlight.

Ephemeral plants

Some plants, called ephemerals, spend most of the time lying in the ground as seeds. When it rains, the seeds burst into life, producing leaves in as little as two hours.

The plants flower briefly, then die, leaving more seeds to lie in wait for the next rains. Ephemerals can produce 1.5 billion seeds per hectare of desert!

Desert in bloom after rain, South Africa.

We're in the chain!

The San people, who live in Africa's Kalahari Desert, eat wild watermelons and cucumbers. The plants are an important source of water and vitamin C.

Yummy!

When ephemeral plants blossom after rain, honey ants feed some of their workers plant nectar until their bodies swell up. The other ants use the swollen workers as food containers, and suck the nectar from them. Honey ants are eaten by lizards, who are in turn eaten by birds of prey, such as hawks.

This huge saguaro cactus grows in the south-western USA.

Perennial plants

Plants that stay alive all the time are called perennials. Desert perennials include tough grasses. In very dry times the grasses look dead but their long roots are still alive under the ground. Other perennials are cactus plants, which grow in North and South America. After it has rained, cacti can store huge amounts of water in their stems, which swell like balloons.

Who Eats Who?

prickly pear (fruit)

worker honey ant

other honey ants eat nectar stored in worker

horned lizard

hawk

Eating it up

The first animal in a food chain is always a herbivore – a plant-eater. Herbivores in the desert range in size from tiny insects to big mammals, such as antelopes and kangaroos.

Small animal food chains

In the driest deserts there are few plants, so herbivores have to eat seeds or bits of plants blown into the desert on the wind. Deserts like this only have enough food for tiny plant-eaters, like insects.

The next animals in food chains are carnivores – meat-eaters. In very dry deserts the carnivores are small spiders or lizards, or small rodents. Other carnivores, such as snakes and birds, eat these animals.

Bigger animal food chains

Deserts with more plant life support larger herbivores. In Africa, deer-like mammals called gazelles get all the food and water they need from desert plants – some species spend their entire lives without drinking water.

Bigger herbivores attract bigger carnivores. Desert animals that hunt gazelles are jackals, hyenas and wild cats called caracals, which have short tails and pointed, tufty ears.

A female kangaroo and her baby, called a joey.

This wily coyote of the south-western USA is an omnivore – it has a varied diet.

Omnivores

Many desert animals are not purely herbivores or carnivores but omnivores – they eat everything! In the Mojave Desert in the USA, wild dogs called coyotes eat rabbits, rodents, antelopes and goats. But they are also happy to eat plants, especially the seed pods of the mesquite tree.

Breaking it down

When a living thing produces waste or dies, animals called decomposers break it down. The broken-down matter then provides nutrients that help plants to grow.

About decomposers

When a plant or animal dies, many animals will not eat it. But micro-organisms such as bacteria and fungi, known as decomposers, attack the dead matter. They eat it and begin to break it down.

In the desert, decomposers include beetles, earthworms and millipedes. These animals feed on dead and decaying bits of plants or animals that they find on or underneath the surface of the desert.

We're in the chain!

In Africa, people fry or roast winged termites, or grind them into a flour. Queen termites, in particular, are considered to be a delicacy.

A termite nest

Termites

Some of the most important desert decomposers are small insects with soft, pale bodies called termites. They look like ants, but are more closely related to cockroaches.

Most termites live underground in groups, called colonies, and eat a variety of dead material. Australian scientists have found that desert termites there eat dead grasses, leaves, roots and wood, and sheep and kangaroo dung.

Smaller decomposers

After beetles, earthworms and termites have eaten the dead plant or animal material, most of it passes out of their bodies into the soil. But now it is in much smaller pieces, ready for even tinier animals to eat.

These micro-organisms include nematode worms and protozoans, which can be less than 0.01 mm long. These decomposers break down this waste, releasing minerals that help new plants grow.

Who Eats Who?

camel dung

scarab beetle

termite (eats beetle's waste)

nematode worm (eats termite's waste)

new plant (helped to grow by minerals released by broken down dung)

Yummy!

African dung beetles gather up the dung of animals, such as camels and goats, and roll it into balls. The beetle buries the ball underground and later feeds off it.

Dung beetle

The desert at night

When the temperature drops at night the desert comes alive with activity. Many animals emerge to look for seeds, nibble at plants or hunt other creatures.

The fennec fox

In the Sahara Desert lives a small mammal weighing less than a pet cat. It is a type of fox called a fennec (right) and it comes out at night to catch lizards, insects and rodents such as gerbils.

The fennec is well adapted to night-time hunting. It has a good sense of smell and huge ears that pick up the tiniest noises of its prey. During the day, the fennec's big ears also help its body heat to escape.

Keeping cool

Mammals are warm-blooded. This means their bodies always stay at the same temperature. Most desert mammals, including rodents, rabbits, foxes and cats, are nocturnal – they are active at night.

The reason for this is that warm-blooded mammals feel comfortable in the chilly desert night, but they can overheat during the day. To avoid this, many animals spend the daytime sleeping in cool underground burrows or beneath rocks.

An angry scorpion holds its tail up, ready to strike.

Yummy!

The ningaui is a tiny rodent that lives in Australia's deserts. It weighs only 4 g, but is an aggressive night hunter. The ningaui's two favourite meals – desert centipedes and cockroaches – are bigger than it is!

Insects, spiders and scorpions

Many smaller desert creatures like flies, ants and grasshoppers, as well as spiders, are also active at night. Scorpions can survive fiercer heat than insects, but they too are nocturnal.

Some scorpions are 12 cm long. They are bold hunters and catch spiders, insects and other scorpions with their powerful pincers, before killing them with the poison stings in their tails. The poison from some scorpions is so strong that it can kill a person in a few hours.

Daytime desert

Daytime desert food chains are made up of animals whose bodies can withstand the scorching, dry heat.

Reptiles rule

The kings of the daytime desert – lizards, snakes and tortoises – are reptiles. Unlike mammals, reptiles are cold-blooded. Their body temperature changes according to their surroundings.

At night, when desert temperatures drop, reptiles lose their body heat and have little energy for hunting. In daytime, however, the heat of the sun warms them up, giving them the energy to look for food.

A blazing daytime desert scene.

Western diamondback rattlesnake

Lizards and tortoises

The largest lizard of all is the desert monitor lizard. It lives in Africa and Asia and grows to 1.6 m. A much smaller lizard is the spiny-tailed lizard of northern Africa, which reaches about 30 cm.

Most lizards and snakes (see pages 18-19) are carnivores, but tortoises are herbivores. The desert tortoise of the USA can store nearly a litre of water in its body just from the plants it eats, and survives on this liquid during dry times.

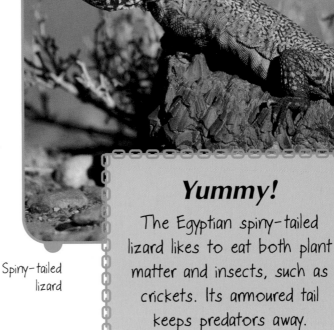

Spiny-tailed lizard

Yummy!

The Egyptian spiny-tailed lizard likes to eat both plant matter and insects, such as crickets. Its armoured tail keeps predators away.

We're in the chain!

Although their traditional ways are becoming much less common, some San people in the Kalahari Desert still hunt animals such as antelope using bows and poisoned arrows, as well as with animal traps.

Daytime mammals

Not all desert mammals come out at night. Many large mammals cope with the heat better than smaller ones and some, like antelopes, camels and kangaroos, are too big to find shelter from the sun.

Antelopes, for example, can withstand increases in their body temperature even though they are warm-blooded. And a camels' thick fur coat actually acts as a shield against the sun.

Who Eats Who?

ant eggs

ant

cricket

elephant shrew

snake

desert monitor lizard

Life in the sand

Sandy desert regions provide animals with a cool place to burrow and hide from the sun. But the sand is not always safe – expert hunters are never far away.

Small sand-dwellers

Smaller creatures that live in the sand include camel crickets, scorpions, beetles, cockroaches and spiders. These animals don't burrow just for the cooler temperatures there, but because they know they may be able to find water beneath the surface, or the remains of plant or animal matter. One fearsome insect that hunts in the sand is the larva of the antlion fly. It digs a pit in the sand, covers itself with more sand and waits for another insect to slide down into the hole and then eats it.

Antlion fly lava

Yummy!

The antlion fly larva paralyzes its prey with poison from its jaws. It then sucks out the insides of its victim and throws the empty skin out of the pit.

Young bearded
dragon lizard

Bigger sand-dwellers

A bigger animal that eats insects that burrow in the sand is the legless skink lizard of Africa's Namib Desert. The skink moves through the sand by wriggling. It once had legs but has lost them through evolution.

In Australia, the bearded dragon lizard grows to about 50 cm. It is an expert hunter, eating all kinds of smaller sand-dwelling creatures.

Snakes

Many snakes are also very good at hunting in the sand but they move across the surface rather than burrowing into it. Sidewinding snakes move by slithering sideways.

The sidewinding adder of the Namib Desert plays a hunting trick. The only part of the snake's body visible above the sand is its tail. It moves its tail to imitate an insect and so attracts unwary lizards.

Life on a plant

Some desert plants are a home to many different animals and contain entire food chains.
This is especially true of the saguaro cactus and the desert ironwood tree, both found in the deserts of the south-western USA.

Saguaro cactus

The saguaro cactus is the tallest of all cactus plants, growing up to 15 m in height. Despite its poisonous, prickly spines, many animals live on or in the saguaro.

Desert woodpeckers make holes in the top of the plant, in which they build nests. Cactus pygmy owls, which are small enough to fit into a person's hand, often move into these nests when woodpeckers have left. The owls hunt other birds, lizards, rodents and insects that live on or near the cactus.

This desert woodpecker nests in a saguaro cactus.

We're in the chain!

Native Americans have traditionally ground up the seeds of the desert ironwood tree and eaten them. They have also used the tree's flowers and roots for medicines.

A cactus pygmy owl and its chicks in their nest in the middle of a saguaro cactus.

Ironwood chain

Desert ironwood trees support around 500 plant and animal species in their native region of the USA's Sonoran Desert. The ironwood's leaves give shade to many creatures. Most years the tree produces hard seed pods, which rodents such as the kangaroo rat like to break open and eat. Kangaroo rats are eaten in their turn by long-nosed snakes, and snakes by kit foxes and other larger mammals.

Helping other plants

The desert ironwood also offers shade to smaller plants, such as cacti and wild flowers, and protects them from cold temperatures at night. The plants that grow underneath ironwoods attract more animals to feed there, including jack rabbits, desert bighorn sheep and deer.

Who Eats Who?

ironwood seeds

kangaroo rat

long-nosed snake

kit fox

From the ground to the air

Birds and flying insects have a big advantage over other desert animals. They can travel farther to hunt whatever food is available.

Desert birds

In Australia, desert birds include brightly-coloured parrots as well as the Australian bustard, which grabs lizards and rodents with its sharp beak and swallows them whole. The roadrunner of the south-western USA (right) prefers to walk rather than fly. It eats insects, scorpions, lizards and even rattlesnakes.

In Africa and the USA, two large birds that often fly over deserts are the golden eagle and the vulture. All eagles kill their own prey, but vultures are scavengers so they look for animals that are dead already.

Cooling down

Because flying creates a lot of heat, birds are used to high body temperatures. Their feathers provide protection from the sun's rays, and many birds also cool down by fluttering the skin on their throats – just like we use a fan.

Reptile snack: a roadrunner devours a lizard.

Locusts gather together in huge swarms.

Locusts

Insects, such as flies, wasps, crickets and butterflies also fly over the desert. But the best-known flying desert insects are locusts. Locusts fly together in huge groups, or swarms, of up to 40 billion.

As they fly, locusts are pulled by low air pressure to places where it has rained and plants are growing. Swarms can eat up all the plants in an area of desert. This can seriously affect food chains and webs for other animals and ruin farm crops.

A watery food chain

Rain showers in the desert cause new life to burst out, and trigger off short-lived food chains. One of these chains involves the amazing spadefoot toad of the Arizona Desert in the USA.

Spadefoot toads

Most toads like damp places, so they are not natural desert dwellers. The spadefoot toad is different. It hides in a burrow that it digs under the ground with its hind feet.

After a rare desert rain shower, the spadefoot emerges into daylight. Male and female toads mate, and the female lays her eggs in a shallow pool that the rain has made.

Race for survival

As soon as the eggs hatch into tadpoles, the race begins for them to grow into adults before their watery home in the pool dries up. This is because an adult toad can live out of water, but a tadpole cannot.

The pools are full of algae, water fleas and tiny shrimp that come to life when it rains. All are food for the tadpoles.

Spadefoot toad

Spadefoot
tadpole

Yummy!
Spadefoot tadpoles make a tasty snack for many lizards, which are in turn eaten by desert birds.

Who Eats Who?

algae

water flea

spadefoot
tadpole

larger spadefoot
tadpole

lizard

roadrunner (bird)

Tadpoles eating tadpoles

The pools can also contain larger shrimps called fairy shrimp. If there are fairy shrimp around, some tadpoles develop bigger heads and mouths to eat them. And the bigger tadpoles don't stop there – they also start to eat the smaller tadpoles too. This means the bigger tadpoles can become toads even more quickly, which might be vital if the pool is fast drying out.

On the edge of the desert

Many deserts are surrounded by grasslands or mountains. While these areas are still hot and dry, they receive more rain than deserts themselves and so attract more plants and animals.

Savannah

On the edge of many deserts lies a region of grasses and scattered trees known as savannah. In Africa, herds of antelope and gazelle often roam this region. But they must stay on the alert for the animals that hunt them, such as lions, leopards, cheetahs and caracals.

Lion

We're in the chain!

As people build more homes and cities on the edge of deserts, so animals adapt to their new surroundings. In cities on the edge of deserts in the south-western USA, for example, coyotes often eat scraps of food from rubbish bins.

Staying together

Many antelopes and gazelles stay in large herds for safety. Most young antelope are born around the same time for the same reason. If they were born throughout the year the big cats would have a constant supply of vulnerable prey.

Many antelope wander deep into the desert, for example after rains, when more plants grow. At such times, lions and other predators follow them, in search of a meal.

Rare rhinoceroses

The region around the Namib Desert in south-west Africa has both flat savannah and high mountains. It is home to many endangered animals, such as the mountain zebra and the black rhinoceros. Like the zebra, the rhinoceros is a herbivore, feeding on grasses and woody plants. Rhinoceroses have few predators – apart from people, who have killed them in large numbers for their horns.

Who Eats Who?

leaf

springbok (antelope)

leopard

A springbok in a South African desert setting.

Yummy!

Birds such as oxpeckers spend a lot of their time on rhinoceroses' backs, eating the small insects that make their home there.

Food web

Here is a typical desert food web, together with some fascinating desert facts.

Deserts and semi-deserts make up nearly one-third of the Earth's land area.

Some desert animals, including fennec foxes and certain scorpions, obtain all the water they need from the animals they kill.

Tortoises

Decomposers
(bacteria and fungi, insects and earthworms, protozoans and nematode worms)

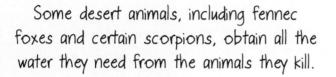

Desert plants
(perennials and ephemerals)

Insects

To find water deep underground, the roots of the camelthorn acacia tree, which grows in African deserts, can reach down 30 m.

The hottest air temperature ever recorded was in the Sahara Desert in Libya in 1922. It was 57.8°C.

Herbivores, mammals and birds

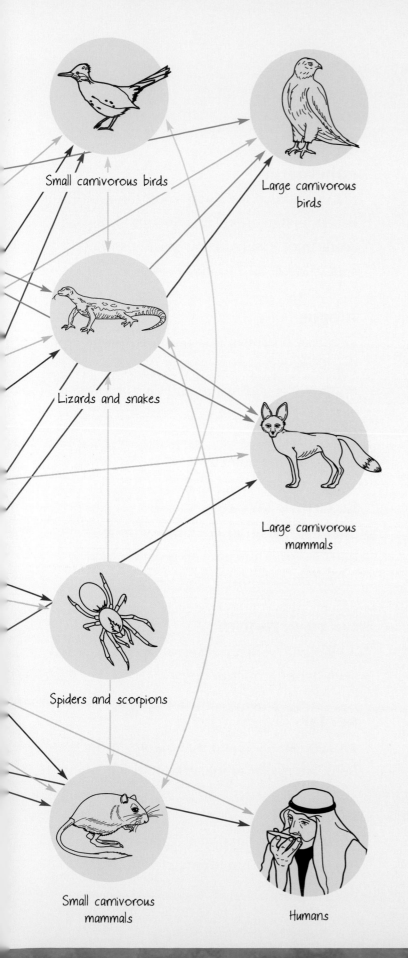

Small carnivorous birds

Large carnivorous birds

Lizards and snakes

Large carnivorous mammals

Spiders and scorpions

Small carnivorous mammals

Humans

The date palm tree is a very important plant for people living in the deserts of North Africa and the Middle East. They eat its fruit (dates), use the wood for houses and the leaves for fences, baskets and sandals.

Fairy shrimp eggs can blow with the desert dust for 50 years before rains cause the shrimp to hatch and grow.

Some bristlecone pine trees, which grow in the deserts of North America, have been alive for about 5,000 years.

Scientists think there are around 1,200 different types of plant in the Sahara Desert and about 40 different kinds of rodent!

Glossary

algae

very simple types of plants that do not have stems, roots or leaves. Most algae live in watery places, but some live in deserts.

bacteria

tiny, one-celled micro-organisms that live in soil, as well as in water, plants and animals' bodies.

carnivore

a meat-eating animal.

cold-blooded

an animal whose body temperature is linked to the outside temperature. At night, when it is cold, cold-blooded animals are also cold. When the sun rises, they warm up. Insects, spiders, fish, amphibians and reptiles are all cold-blooded.

decomposer

a living thing that feeds on and breaks down dead plants and animals as well as animal waste.

desert

a region with few plants and trees, where it rarely rains. One definition of a desert is a place that receives less than 25 cm of rain each year.

ephemerals

plants that live for a very short time. In the desert, ephemeral plants remain lifeless as seeds until it rains. They quickly sprout roots, flower and produce seeds.

fungus

a type of organism (the plural is "fungi") that lives on dead or rotting things. Mould, mushrooms and rust are all types of fungus.

herbivore

a plant-eating animal.

larva (pl. larvae)

the form that an insect takes when it hatches from an egg. Larvae often look very different from adult insects.

micro-organism

a living thing that is so small it can only be seen under a microscope.

nectar

a sweet, sticky liquid that plants produce. Bees use nectar to make honey.

nocturnal

describes an animal that comes out at night to eat and perform other activities, such as hunting.

nomad

a member of a group of people who move their home from place to place, in search of good land on which their herds of animals can feed.

omnivore

an animal that eats plants and other animals. Many desert animals are omnivores.

perennials

plants that survive all year round, and sometimes for many, many years. Some desert perennial plants are around 5,000 years old.

photosynthesis

the process by which plants capture the energy of sunlight to make sugar.

pollen

tiny, dust-like specks in a flower that make plant seeds grow.

predator

an animal that kills and eats other animals.

savannah

an area of grassland that contains scattered trees or bushes. Some savannah regions are on the edge of deserts.

scavenger

an animal that eats dead or dying things. Decomposers are scavengers, but the best-known are vultures.

warm-blooded

animals that maintain the same body temperature when it is hot or cold outside.

Desert websites

www.oxfam.org.uk/coolplanet/ontheline/explore/nature/deserts/deserts.htm
Informative site – a collaboration between Oxfam UK, WWF-UK and Channel 4.

www.ucmp.berkeley.edu/glossary/gloss5/biome/deserts.html
All about deserts, from the University of California at Berkeley.

http://digital-desert.com/wildlife/
Lots of good information about US desert wildlife.

Index